TRUTHFILLED

The Practice of Preaching to Yourself Through Every Season

Ruth Chou Simons

Published by Lifeway Press® • © 2022 Ruth Chou Simons

ISBN: 978-1-0877-7390-2 • Item: 005839459

Dewey decimal classification: 227.7
Subject headings: BIBLE. N.T. COLOSSIANS—STUDY AND TEACHING / TRUTH / CHRISTIAN LIFE

To order additional copies of this resource, write to Lifeway Resources Customer Service; One Lifeway Plaza; Nashville, TN 37234; order online at lifeway.com; fax 615.251.5933; phone toll free 800.458.2772; or email orderentry@lifeway.com.

Printed in the United States of America

Lifeway Women Bible Studies,
Lifeway Resources,
One Lifeway Plaza,
Nashville, TN 37234

EDITORIAL TEAM,
LIFEWAY WOMEN
BIBLE STUDIES

Becky Loyd
Director, Lifeway Women

Tina Boesch
Manager

Sarah Doss
Editorial Project Leader

Elizabeth Hyndman
Content Editor

Erin Franklin
Production Editor

Lauren Ervin
Graphic Designer

CONTENTS

ABOUT THE AUTHOR

Ruth Chou Simons is a bestselling and award-winning author of several books—including *GraceLaced, Beholding and Becoming, Foundations,* and *When Strivings Cease.* She is an artist, entrepreneur, and speaker, using each of these platforms to spiritually sow the Word of God into people's hearts. Ruth is the watercolorist and artist behind GraceLaced.com, a popular brand and retail website that features her unique style of art paired with biblical truth in prints, stationery, and lifestyle products, which reaches a wide audience each month with beauty and truth. Through her ministry, business, writing, and social media community,   Ruth shares her journey of God's grace intersecting daily life. Ruth and her husband, Troy, are grateful parents to six boys—their greatest adventure.

DEAR FRIENDS,

I live in Western Colorado where the seasons are pronounced and intensely vibrant. When it snows here, we get eight inches in a few hours! In spring, all the birds and buds burst forth to meet us as if they couldn't wait to be done with the cold as well. When it's summer, the wildflowers cover an entire hillside. And when the leaves turn here in the mountains, they make a bold statement with waves of gold and blazing shades of orange. If you've never experienced these seasons, be sure to make a visit—you won't be disappointed.

I can't help but think in imagery as an artist as I look out my window and see the similarities between the seasons that occur in creation and the seasons of my heart. Winter, with its waiting and wondering if anything will ever change or grow, spring, with its promises of tender shoots and new blooms, summer, exploding with fruit and evidence of growth, fall, heavy with harvest and ready for rest.

In my 2017 book, *GraceLaced: Discovering Timeless Truths Through Seasons of the Heart*, I wrote devotions to accompany these seasons—seasons of growth, loss, fruitfulness, and weariness that we navigate as believers. I love hearing how those meditations in *GraceLaced* have encouraged and inspired you as readers. In those pages, I suggested through art and writing that we can respond to each season with one of four reminders of our hope in Christ—a response appropriate for the season we're in:

Winter . . . Rest in His Character

Spring . . . Rehearse Your Identity in Christ

Summer . . . Respond in Faith

Fall . . . Remember His Provision[1]

As you and I begin this journey here in the *TruthFilled* study, my goal is to show you the why and how behind preaching these truths—of God's character, our identity in Christ, our response in faith, and our provision for endurance—back to ourselves, whatever season we're in.

We will use the Book of Colossians to walk through the pattern and practice of preaching truth to ourselves as Paul set the example for what we preach to ourselves. The practice of preaching truth to yourself isn't an easy fix, a form of self-help, or a formula for success. It's meeting your perennial trials and challenges of faith with the truth of what is unchanging in Christ.

I can't wait to grow together, replacing what naturally fills our hearts and minds with biblical truth that will both fulfill and satisfy us like nothing else.

Here's to being truth-filled.

Ruth Chou Simons

HOW TO USE THIS STUDY

I'm so grateful you're learning with me what it means to preach truth to your own heart. It is such a privilege to come along on this journey with you as we study God's Word, reminding ourselves who He is and who we are because of Him.

This study may be structured a little differently than studies you've done in the past, so I wanted to take a moment to explain how to use it. This study is meant to be just that—a place for you to study Scripture, jot down questions and answers and prayers, and chart how God is using His Word to teach you more about His heart. I would encourage you to get a group of friends together to walk through this study. When we join hands and walk through the Bible in community, we're reminded of the God who is with us and His commands to care for one another. We have the opportunity to witness His work in the lives of our friends and be reminded of His work in our own lives as well. Encourage and challenge one another as you grow and dwell on the truth.

In each session, you'll find a video viewer guide and sections of personal study. Because this study is going to ask you to put into practice what we're learning, I broke the sessions up in sections instead of days. My hope is that this encourages you to take time where you need to hang out a bit longer and dive deep into the truth of Scripture. You can choose when and how long you spend on each section—completing all of them at once, or a little each day, according to your personality and schedule.

VIDEOS AND VIEWER GUIDES

Your copy of *TruthFilled* comes with streaming access to the videos. You'll find detailed instructions for how to view them on the card inserted in the back of your Bible study book.

You'll also find video viewer guides before each session, with a few questions to guide your discussion if you're doing this study with a group. The questions will both review the previous week's study as well as ask for feedback about the video teaching. Feel free to use these or to make up your own discussion questions! You know your group best; use these as a starting point if you get stuck.

The order of the study is intended for groups to meet together first, watch the first video session, and then do the first session of personal study. The next week, you'll review the last session's personal study, watch the next video teaching session, and then preview the next week's topic in discussion. If your group chooses to watch the videos on their own, you'll just want to spend a bit more time reviewing the previous week's personal study.

During this study, you'll be invited to practice preaching truth to yourself every week. I am praying you'll step up to the challenge and your heart will fall even more deeply in love with our God—the Source of the truth with which we seek to be filled.

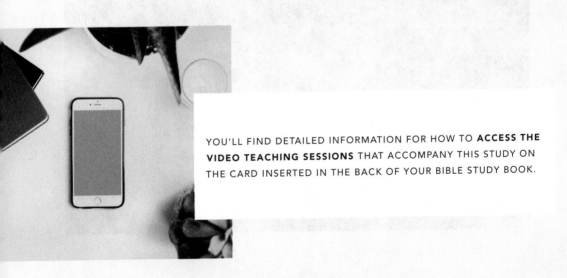

YOU'LL FIND DETAILED INFORMATION FOR HOW TO **ACCESS THE VIDEO TEACHING SESSIONS** THAT ACCOMPANY THIS STUDY ON THE CARD INSERTED IN THE BACK OF YOUR BIBLE STUDY BOOK.

SESSION ONE | INTRODUCTION

INTRODUCTION

COLOSSIANS *1:1 - 14*

14

Do not be conformed to this world, but be transformed by the renewal of your mind, that by testing you may discern what is the will of God, what is good and acceptable and perfect.

ROMANS 12:2

Notes

WELCOME

As we begin, discuss the following questions with your group:

What drew you to this study?

What words would you use to describe your relationship with God's Word?

Share with the group something you hope to learn from this study.

WATCH THE VIDEO

Feel free to use the space on the previous page to jot down notes as you watch Ruth's video teaching.

DISCUSS

Take a few moments to think through these questions from the video teaching or discuss them with your small group.

When have you found yourself, "like a wave of the sea, blown and tossed by the wind" (Jas. 1:6, NIV) in the circumstances of life? In those moments, how do you typically respond?

In the moments when you allow yourself to spin out of control instead of binding yourself to the Lord in truth, what might be keeping you from trusting the Lord over your own heart?

Is there a specific lie in relation to God or yourself that you continually have to preach truth to your heart about? If you feel comfortable, share it with a friend or your small group.

What truth from God's Word would directly apply to the lie that you mentioned above?

Close your time in prayer, thanking God for the truth of His Word and asking Him to give you the grace to preach truth to your own heart this week, moment by moment, day by day.

TO ACCESS THE VIDEO TEACHING SESSIONS,
USE THE INSTRUCTIONS IN THE BACK OF YOUR BIBLE STUDY BOOK.

TRUTHFILLED

If I were to ask you who your greatest influences are, you might cite your hardworking father, your witty grandmother, or maybe your eleventh grade history teacher. Perhaps you'd think of a mentor, pastor, or close friend.

But Paul David Tripp tells it to us straight, saying, "no one is more influential in your life than you are, because no one talks to you more than you do."[1] Oh, how true this is. Turns out we are more influential in our own lives than we realize. Just one quick inventory of the thoughts that dominated our thinking this day can leave us confronted with the truth: We are what we think.

What are some of the thoughts that go through your mind in the day-to-day? Here are some of mine, even now:

I'll never change—I'll never overcome this weakness. I'm not a good mom—I'll ruin these kids. I'm not capable of this difficult task. I shouldn't trust people—I'll inevitably get hurt. I should be so much further along in my walk with the Lord—God must be disappointed in me. I can't minister or lead if I don't have all the answers. I wouldn't be going through these circumstances if I were a better Christian.

My guess is that while those statements seem recognizable as lies when someone else says them, you too allow them to form in your mind about yourself and your own circumstances. See how much your thoughts direct your days? Can you see why Tripp says no one is more influential than you are?

Proverbs 23:7 says, "For as he thinks in his heart, so is he" (NKJV).

The principle here is that your heart and your mind are connected. You can try to act or behave in a certain way, but ultimately, your actions will take the shape of what drives our hearts and minds.

Take an inventory. What are the most common thoughts that fill your mind in the day-to-day?

You see, this conviction to meet the jumbled-up thoughts and lies in my mind with the truth of God's Word didn't form out of a noble pursuit of spiritual discipline, but rather through the most brutal of seasons where my emotions and feelings about my life threatened to pull me under the tide of life's unexpected waves of doubt, fear, exhaustion, and disappointment.

Maybe you know what "unexpected" feels like. Most of us intentionally or unintentionally write narratives for our ideal lives that include graduating college with very little school debt and marrying a godly man who will not only be handsome eternally but will also always read our minds when we have needs and always have the right answer for how to lead us into the future. We write scripts for our lives that perhaps include adventures abroad, a good job, nice benefits, a squad of fun friends who will never betray us, a vibrant church to plug into, and lots of opportunities to use our gifts in ways that feel natural and encouraging.

None of us plan to write confusion or failure or chapters of loss, pain, conflict, or suffering into our stories. No one plans to struggle to love her husband, to feel helpless in motherhood, to feel lonely in ministry, to wrestle with identity. But there I was in my late twenties, chaffing from all this and more. In that time of my life, I was in a pattern of bowing to my emotions and stumbling about in my doubt—like James says—"like a wave of the sea, blown and tossed by the wind" (Jas. 1:6, NIV).

My husband Troy and I were both believers, but reality pressed in with the tension of our faith against the pressures of life. And he said to me one day, in the midst of me feeling sorry for myself and in a slump:

"Honey, you really need to preach truth to yourself. You believe the gospel and the hope we have in Christ. Tell yourself what to do like the psalmist does."

The psalm he referred to is Psalm 42.

Read Psalm 42:5-11.

Whom was the psalmist addressing in these verses?

What was the state of the psalmist's heart as he questioned himself?

What were some things he honestly confessed regarding . . .

HIS FEARS?	
HIS PHYSICAL PAIN?	
HIS SADNESS?	

What did he tell his own soul to do?

If the psalmist's remedy for a downcast soul was to tell his soul to put his hope in God, then we must know why putting our hope in Jesus changes our hearts and minds. Somehow as believers we trust Jesus to save us from our sins, but we so easily forget He saves us to a new way of thinking, living, and being.

We may be familiar with Paul's exhortation in Romans 12:2—"Do not conform to the pattern of this world, but be transformed by the renewing of your mind. Then you will be able to test and approve what God's will is—his good, pleasing and perfect will" (NIV)—but so often we try to figure out what God wants to do with our lives by comparing the patterns to success, productivity, or happiness we see in the world.

Describe some formulas or patterns the world prescribes . . .

FOR SUCCESS:

FOR LOVE AND
COMPANIONSHIP:

FOR SECURITY:

FOR PHYSICAL HEALTH:

FOR ACCEPTANCE:

Read Romans 12:2 again.

How did Paul say we are transformed?

Describe what it looks like to renew your mind.

We are transformed by the renewing of our minds. We renew our minds by developing new patterns. Instead of bowing to the pattern of my feelings or my old thoughts, I worked to practice a pattern of preaching truth from God's Word to my own heart, like the psalmist did.

Over the next few weeks, we'll practice this new pattern together. Only by being filled with truth can we be transformed by the renewing of our minds.

Father, help us to rightly assess the deceitful patterns in our minds, the false notions, lies, and inadequate substitutes to being truly renewed of mind in You. So, Lord, as we begin establishing new patterns of belief and thought, change our hearts. Help us to study Your Word, open the eyes of our hearts that we might understand it, and teach us to speak it back to ourselves, in and through every season. Amen.

PAUL'S PATTERN: INDICATIVES VERSUS IMPERATIVES

Have you ever started doing things or buying things in winter in hopes that spring will come more quickly—like when I walk into The Home Depot® and involuntarily reach for all the tiny tomato plants and cucumbers even when snow is still falling?

The other day I saw a huge indoor pot of lettuces growing—and naturally believed I needed to buy a pretty container of lettuce—because what could be more spring-welcoming than to snip lettuce that's growing up from dirt? (I act as if growing veggies on my windowsill will cause snow to melt.)

My boys have their version of this. (You may know that I'm mom to six boys!) They have a habit of putting on sandals and shorts any time the sun is out and the temp reaches above forty degrees Fahrenheit. They start pulling out their summer clothes, bike helmets, and swim trunks. They are ready to be summer people—to do summery things. But the truth is, no matter how diligent they are to wear sandals or how many garden plants I'm ready to plant, we won't be involved with the affairs of summer until the snow melts away and the true changes of the season occur.

You see, the truth is: True change only happens after our state of being changes.

Just like putting on sandals in snow or snipping lettuce from a container in your kitchen has no power to bring on spring, neither does our striving change our hearts apart from gospel transformation.

If you're like me, sometimes it's tempting to want to jump straight into the dos and don'ts of how we should live and skip over the reminders of who God is and who we are in Christ. (Do you sometimes think it is repetitive and maybe even a little boring?)

Read Colossians 3:1-2.

What part of this passage do you immediately respond to?

What do these two verses tell us about who Christ is?

What do these two verses show us to do in response?

I'm tempted to focus on how I must set my mind on things above and dismiss the reminder that the power to do so comes from being raised with Christ as a born-again believer.

A fancy word for right conduct or practice is the word *orthopraxy*[2]—*ortho* meaning straight,[3] *praxy* meaning practice[4] (or *imperatives*). *Orthopraxy* is what we do because of our faith, and *orthodoxy* (or *indicatives*) is what we believe.[5] *Orthodoxy* tells us what is straight; *orthopraxy* tells us how to walk along that straight line.

Without the indicatives—or what is true about who God is and what He's done—the imperatives would be basically impossible. Attempting to do great things for God without trusting in the great things He's already done for us will always lead to either a whole lot of self-righteousness or total despair and distance from God, fearing that you've failed Him.

Right believing leads to right living, so let's grow in the practice of believing and preaching the truth of God's Word to ourselves, together.

WHY COLOSSIANS?

The apostle Paul wrote Colossians to the church of Colossae—what we now know as a part of modern day Turkey.[6] Paul wrote the letter while in prison in Rome. News reached Paul that heresy was swarming around the church at Colossae and threatened to influence the believers there with worldly belief systems. Paul wrote to warn the Colossians and direct them to truth in the face of heresy in Colossae. The church at Colossae was a mixture of Jewish and Gentile believers, and though they had heard the truth of the gospel, they were in danger of caving to paganism, worldliness, and the false beliefs in philosophical and legalistic thought.

The lie that threatened the Colossians was simply the idea that Christ was not sufficient—that He alone was not enough. Paul sought to reestablish the truth with his letter: Christ is all.

Paul sought to encourage the believers in Colossae to passionately serve and follow after Christ, but in order to do so, they had to hold steadfastly to be filled by the truth of who God is, who we are in Him, what we must do in response, and how to persevere in the truth as a Christ-follower.

Paul knew that to be filled with the truth of the gospel isn't a one-time outward adherence or acknowledgment, but a daily clinging to what is true while discerning what is false.

Through studying the Book of Colossians, we will also learn to establish a pattern of becoming truth-filled.

How often, in the face of doubt and fear, do we forget the truth that Christ is sufficient?

Like the Colossians, how can you know the gospel and yet become swayed by the persuasive philosophies and messages from the world?

Name some of the ways in which current books, entertainment, media, or pop culture tell us Jesus is not enough.

Assess and confess: How are you, at times . . .

FORGETFUL THAT
JESUS IS GOD AND IS
OUR SUFFICIENCY?

FORGETFUL THAT
WE DO NOT NEED
TO PROVE OUR OWN
SUFFICIENCY?

BEGIN WITH WHAT WE KNOW

Knowing who God is and what He has really done for us is the foundation to any truth we preach to ourselves. How can we believe what He says about us or what He promises for the days to come if we don't first trust what He says about Himself? Paul began his letter to the Colossians with a clear reminder of what they already knew.

Friend, you may feel like you already know these truths as well, but I encourage you to slow down and encounter them anew.

Read Colossians 1:1-14.

As we've already learned, letters were the primary form of communication in Paul's day. Important warnings, praise, exhortation, and instruction were sent as letters and read aloud to the churches during Paul's imprisonment and times when he was unable to visit the churches himself. Paul penned this letter to the Colossians beginning with greetings from himself and Timothy, Paul's mentee and missionary companion.

Imagine the whole church gathered together to hear a word of encouragement from a hero of their faith. This was personal, special, and carried the weight of a personal visit and the authority of a leader who had trained their own pastor. The church in Colossae was founded by Epaphras, a colaborer in the gospel, from whom they learned the gospel (v. 7).

It's clear from reading the letter's introduction that the Colossians' love for one another and for the Lord encouraged Paul.

THE GOAL—TO BE FILLED AND TO WALK IN A MANNER WORTHY

The word *worthy* comes from the root word that means *a balancing of scales*—as in with business transactions—that what is paid matches the work that's being done.[7] Another way to put it: that our lives would correspond appropriately to the measure of position and calling we've been given as followers of Christ.

We can never pay back or earn what salvation in Christ has purchased for us—that's not what was being said here. Instead, Paul was saying that if you are filled with the truth of God's wisdom and understanding, your living will match that fullness and bear fruit.

We don't walk in a worthy manner to *get* saved; we walk in a worthy manner because we *are* saved.

Paul knew that in order to encourage the Colossians to stand firm and "walk in a manner worthy of the Lord" (v. 10), he must remind them to be fueled by what made them worthy in the first place.

Does our everyday living match our inheritance in Christ (v. 12)? Paul, in just the introduction and greetings of his letter, sought to unpack the truths of that inheritance and that redemption for their recollection.

What are some phrases Paul used to define and describe the gospel (vv. 5-6)?

Why is it so important that we know the truth of the grace of God and not subtle counterfeits?

Name some close-but-not-quite versions of the grace of God that can be found in popular culture.

Look at verses 9 and 10: ". . . be filled with the knowledge of His will in all wisdom and spiritual understanding . . . increasing in the knowledge of God" (NKJV).

The word for *filled* here is *plēroō*, meaning more than just filled up: consumed, controlled, completely overtaken.[8] Have you ever noticed how, when you are fully satisfied after a meal, even the most tempting dessert loses its appeal?

In the same way, we make little room for false belief, counterfeit faith, or unfruitful self-help strategies when we are filled up with the truth.

Paul encouraged similarly in his letter to the Ephesians:

> **Then we will no longer be infants, tossed back and forth by the waves, and blown here and there by every wind of teaching and by the cunning and craftiness of people in their deceitful scheming.**
>
> **EPHESIANS 4:14, NIV**

Preaching the truth of the gospel and our knowledge of God's Word isn't rooted in storing up more information. It is to be deeply rooted in truths that you can quickly recall when seasons are tumultuous, tender, or difficult to discern. We won't be swept away by wrong thinking when we are maturing in right believing.

Read Colossians 1:10-11 again.

According to Paul, what accompanies being filled with the knowledge of God with wisdom and understanding?

Reread Colossians 1:12.

We will certainly look more at how we are sons and daughters, why we are "qualified . . . to share in the inheritance" when we get to the second pattern next week—preaching to ourselves the truth of who we are in Christ. But for now, let's focus on the gift Paul wanted his readers to remember. We see it in other places in the New Testament, too.

Read Ephesians 1:11-14 and 1 Peter 1:4.

What do these verses, along with Colossians 1:12, show us about our inheritance in Christ?

Reread Colossians 1:1-14 and answer the following questions based on what you see in those verses:

What is true about God?

What is true about Christ?

What has He done for us?

What have we been given?

HOW TO WRITE A SERMON
TO PREACH TO YOUR OWN HEART

We're going to practice preaching to ourselves week-by-week. A good sermon preached to your own heart takes practice, and it takes content! It's not preaching truth to yourself if you're not filled up with the truth. Let's try and construct a sermon to preach to ourselves, together:

1   **Identify the care.** What's the issue? "Why are you downcast?" (Ps. 42:5, BSB).

     Write out what your concern is.

     For example: I'm overwhelmed by my to-do list.

2   **Tell your soul what to do.** "Put your hope in God" (Ps. 42:5, BSB).

How? You put your hope in God by looking to the Word and recounting the hope of the gospel and the character of Christ.

The psalmist, David, showed us in Psalm 103 how to preach a sermon to ourselves. He told himself how to keep his eyes on his Father rather than his circumstances by recounting what God has done, what's true about His character, and why he can trust Him.

Read all of Psalm 103.

Let's look more closely at verse 2.

> Bless the LORD, O my soul, and forget not all his benefits.
>
> PSALM 103:2

To "forget not all his benefits" is to rehearse God's faithfulness instead of your fears, to praise Him instead of pouting, and to humble yourself as a child who trusts in her Father instead of herself.

Write out some of God's benefits, His character, and what's true about Christ and our hope in Him.

For example: Jesus paid every debt I owe as a sinner. He doesn't just save me *from* guilt and condemnation; He saves me *to* freedom and eternal joy. I'm qualified for my inheritance in Christ (Col. 1:12). He delivered me from darkness to light (v. 13) and has forgiven my sins (v. 14). This is how I'm able to "walk in a manner worthy" of Him and bear fruit (v. 10).

Embrace gospel hope. How does the good news of Christ (the gospel) change your perspective?

Preach the sermon to yourself and write out how Jesus satisfies—at the core—the concerns of your heart.

For example: I'm overwhelmed by my to-do list. But because Jesus, on the cross, fulfilled every requirement ever needed to be acceptable in God's sight, I do not have to look at my to-do list as a means of securing acceptance or freedom. Jesus has already secured those things for me, and in Christ, I can pursue my to-do lists as someone approved, not needing approval. The Bible tells me that "His divine power has given us everything required for life and godliness through

the knowledge of him who called us by his own glory and goodness"
(2 Pet. 1:3, CSB). That means I have everything I need to do all that
He's given me to do, by His power.

The work God has accomplished through Christ, to secure eternal hope for us, His children, is the most important sermon we can preach to ourselves. It is the foundational truth upon which we rest everything else we believe about who we are and what He has for us to do. It's the only fuel that will drive our efforts to obey, serve, or be fruitful in our faith. And when we believe God is who He says He is, we also have the basis for the truths of how He will sustain us to the end.

PRACTICE THE PATTERN

So as we finish this week's study, consider how you can preach or counsel your heart with these truths of who God is and what He's done for us, right in the midst of your current circumstance in these areas.

I am filled.

God satisfies me with truth and grace.

1   **In what current circumstance do you feel weary and lacking strength?**

2   **Preach it to yourself:**

Because grace is mine through Jesus (Col. 1:6), and He is the substance of true knowledge (vv. 9-10) and hope (v. 14), I don't need to be filled up with any other counterfeit in my life.

3 Practice writing your own:

_____

_____

_____

_____

_____

_____

I have an inheritance.

God has eternal treasure and hope for me.

1 In what current circumstance do you think you're lacking all you need?

2 Preach it to yourself:

Because of Jesus, I'm given an inheritance that will not fade, can't be lost, and isn't dependent on impressing everyone around me. I don't need to put my hope in what I can achieve, acquire, or produce today (v. 12).

3 Practice writing your own:

_____

_____

_____

_____

_____

SESSION TWO | WINTER

REST
IN GOD'S
CHARACTER

COLOSSIANS 1:15–2:3

Running behind and running on empty—sometimes we find our sense of hope trampled on the hardened earth of a winter season in our lives. God calls us to lay down our frantic striving and fears to discover what might be in store for us as we wait, trust, weep, and rest.

GRACELACED, WINTER[1]

Notes

WELCOME

As we begin, discuss the following questions with your group:

Read Colossians 3:1-2 together aloud. Discuss what the passage tells us about Christ and what we are to do.

What did you learn about God in Colossians 1:1-14 this week? (See the questions on the bottom of p. 31 if you need to refresh your memory.)

Which of the three pieces of writing a sermon for your own heart (identifying the issue, telling your soul what to do, and embracing gospel hope) comes the most naturally to you? Which is the most challenging?

WATCH THE VIDEO

Feel free to use the space on the previous page to jot down notes as you watch Ruth's video teaching.

DISCUSS

Take a few moments to think through these questions from the video teaching or discuss them with your small group.

Take a moment to consider: Who or what are you listening to most consistently? It could be a friend, social media, a pastor, or maybe a spouse. What kinds of messages do you hear from them?

When you hear the phrase "tell your soul what to do" what comes to mind? Does it seem like an easy practice, or do you find yourself a bit intimidated? Explain.

Do you sometimes strive for fruit while ignoring the roots? Discuss why and how this can happen.

In our video time together, we discussed how we can't know how to walk our Christ-ward walk without first knowing who enables that walk. This week, take some time to intentionally meditate over the attributes of God and take time to stand in awe of who He is.

TO ACCESS THE VIDEO TEACHING SESSIONS,
USE THE INSTRUCTIONS IN THE BACK OF YOUR BIBLE STUDY BOOK.

TRUTHFILLED

Our family moved to Colorado a few years ago in the middle of winter. It was practically a blizzard on the day we arrived with two giant U-Haul® trucks. Friends and family gathered in the blowing wind and snow to help us unload appliances, furniture, and all the ridiculous things that you stuff in at the very last minute. It was comical, if not a little dangerous, as all of us slid on the icy driveway. A few weeks later, the snow began to melt and revealed a brown patch of dirt in front of the entry to our home. We had purchased the house and moved, all in wintertime, so I had never really noticed this area. It was brown, with a couple rocks here and there. Was it a flower bed? I didn't know. Were there bulbs planted, seeds sown, perennials that would come up year after year? I couldn't tell because the path didn't look like flowers, smell like flowers, or even seem capable of producing flowers.

You see, in winter seasons of our lives, unless we're the ones who sowed and watered and cultivated the soil, we can't tell that there's anything growing. We have to wait. In winter, we're tempted to think that nothing will ever change.

The winter season of the heart is the waiting season, the season of goodbyes, the season of losses, and the season when we're just not sure if we'll survive the bitter cold. In this season, I think of the psalmist David, when he was afraid for his life and unsure of his future. And just as we see in the psalms he wrote, we must rest in the character of God in a wintry season of the heart because it is God who is at work in the unseen, beneath the surface, behind the seemingly impossible.

Resting is not passive here. When we rest in the character of God and in the work of Christ, we actively choose to cease striving in light of who our Savior is.

The Bible tells us God is sovereign, wise, and good. So the most impossibly bleak situations are God's platform to reveal the rest we can only have in Him. Let's look, together, at why Jesus is trustworthy and more than sufficient for us to rest in. But first, a moment in prayer.

Lord, thank You for Your goodness to us and Your faithfulness to work in and through us, even when we can't always see what You are doing. Please open our eyes to see the truth of Your Word and character here. Amen.

PREACH THE TRUTH OF WHO HE IS

Read Colossians 1:15–2:3.

We are focusing this week on the character of God and the worthiness of Christ, beginning with the foundational truths found in Colossians 1–2. As we follow the apostle Paul's Romans 12 pattern of renewing our minds, we'll see his pattern begins with reminders of who Christ is before diving into how to live for Him.

As we've already learned, the Colossians were in danger of believing heretical ideas about Jesus. One of those heresies surrounding the church was the rejection of Christ's true identity as God Himself.

Why is it important that we believe who Christ says He is before we attempt to believe what He says about us or what we are to do in response?

If we don't rest—or fully trust—in God's character or who He says He is, we won't believe anything else He says in His Word. The apostle Paul recognized this and began his letter to the Colossians with a clear picture of the true identity and deity of Christ.

Reread Colossians 1:15-20.

What a bio! What is your main impression of Jesus Christ when you read these verses?

Complete each description given to Christ below:

He is the _____ of the invisible God (v. 15).

He is the _____ of all creation (v. 15).

He is the _____ of all things (v. 16).

He _____ all things together (v. 17).

He is the _____ of the church (v. 18).

He is the _____ (v. 18).

He has _____ place in everything (v. 18).

He possesses the _____ of God (v. 19).

He reconciles _____ things to himself (v. 20).

He made _____ by the blood of His cross (v. 20).

Now look up each coordinating, cross-reference Scripture. In light of what you read in each passage below, rewrite each descriptor of Jesus in your own words.

Image of the Invisible God: Hebrews 1:3

Firstborn of All Creation: Romans 8:29

Creator of All Things: John 1:3

Holds All Things Together: Hebrews 1:3

Head of the Church: Ephesians 1:22

The Beginning: John 1:1; Ephesians 1:4

First Place: Philippians 2:8-11

Fullness of God: John 10:30

Reconciler: Romans 5:10; 1 John 2:2

Peacemaker: Ephesians 2:14

It's easy to think of ourselves as the heroes of our own stories. It's tempting to believe ourselves able to control all things—until we stop to consider who God says He is.

From the descriptions of Christ we just discussed, which reminder of who Jesus is surprises you? Comforts you? Humbles you?

A. W. Tozer said:

> What comes into our minds when we think about God is the most important thing about us. . . . We tend by a secret law of the soul to move toward our mental image of God.[2]

What comes to your mind about God . . .

WHEN YOU'VE RECEIVED
A DIFFICULT HEALTH
DIAGNOSIS?

WHEN YOU GET A
PROMOTION AT WORK?

WHEN YOUR KIDS ARE
DISOBEDIENT?

WHEN YOU SEE
SUFFERING IN
THE WORLD?

WHEN YOU FEEL
DISCOURAGED?

Below, list a few situations and decisions, both good and bad, that you've walked through this past week.

Now, look at your list. If you had to describe God based on those circumstances, apart from Scripture, how would you view Him? Describe Him below. What's He like?

Look at your list again. If you had to describe God based on those circumstances, but this time allowed the things that the Bible says about God to inform your perspective, how would you view Him? Describe Him below. What's He like?

Compare the two. How does your view of God change by bringing biblical truths to bear on your everyday life?

Is it normally easy or difficult for you to believe that God cares about your everyday life and your needs—both big and small, spiritual and ordinary? Explain.

Below, list a few things that you really think you need—they can be spiritual, physical, or emotional. Anything is fair game.

Are you needing rest, relief, or renewal? Me too. We are made to find our rest in the person of Christ. We must preach to ourselves the truth of who He is, why He is trustworthy, and how He is sufficient for our every spiritual and physical need. Augustine famously voiced our true condition, ". . . Thou madest us for Thyself, and our heart is restless, until it repose in Thee."[3]

Let's pray and ask Him for help as we learn to rest in Him.

Feel free to use the space below to journal a prayer.

KNOWING HIS HEART

Read Colossians 1:21-23.

It's easy to turn to "helpful" passages in our Bibles, encouraging words for a motivational pep talk, or quick reminders that we are loved today. Are you ever tempted to think the gospel exists to help you have a better life, happier relationships, or a more positive attitude? Our hope and redemption in Christ can certainly make us more optimistic, but that was not God's primary goal in sending Jesus to be our Savior.

Paul followed the previous section of his letter, all about the person of Christ, with an exploration of Christ's true motivation.

According to Paul, what is Jesus' stated purpose in reconciling believers to Himself (v. 22)?

What does Jesus' purposeful reconciliation of believers tell you about God?

The picture of Jesus' desire to "present you holy and blameless and above reproach before him" is one of sacrifice, honor, love, and protection. Jesus' sacrifice on the cross made a way for you to know God intimately. And one day you, as a believer in Christ, will be part of the bride of Christ, the church, presented blameless to Jesus at His second coming. He sacrificed greatly for you to know Him because He loves you dearly.

Are your thoughts consumed and filled up with a Savior who has pursued you in this way? Explain your answer.

We—being "hostile in mind" (v. 21)—are incapable of the greatest commandment, "You shall love the Lord your God with all your heart and with all your soul and with all your mind" (Matt. 22:37), without Jesus plucking us from our alienated state and reconciling us to Himself.

Becoming truth-filled and setting our minds on the character of God (and loving Him for who He is!) are not things we can muster up and strategize. They are the works of God! So again, we fix our eyes on how His purposes are to accomplish what we cannot do for ourselves. What a loving Savior!

How were you "hostile in mind" and alienated from God apart from Christ? How is your mind "prone to wander" as the writer of the beloved hymn "Come, Thou Fount" expresses?[4] Pen a prayer thanking Jesus for His work to reconcile you to Himself. Thank Him for His work to present you holy and blameless before Him. Write out how remembering what He's done for you affects your desire to follow and obey Him.

Now, read verse 22 again, this time focusing on what God's faithfulness through Christ purchased for you. (Yes—this is a teaser as we head into next week's study!)

Let's take a few minutes to understand what exactly Christ has purchased for us by unpacking the adjectives Paul used to describe how we'll be seen by Jesus when presented before Him. (These descriptions are not necessarily words we use in our everyday conversations, so it might help to break them down a bit.)

Holy

Read 2 Corinthians 5:21.

Based on this passage, what do we know about God?

What do we learn about ourselves?

Blameless

Read Hebrews 9:14.

Based on this passage, what do we know about God?

What do we learn about ourselves?

Beyond Reproach

Read Romans 8:33-39.

Based on this passage, what do we know about God?

What do we learn about ourselves?

You may have noticed a common thread as you were reading these passages. In every instance, Jesus already has or is each and every thing He's purchased for us. He is sinless and blameless; He is holy and beyond reproach. Because of Him, we can be too. What a glorious truth! Why wouldn't we want to fill our minds with the sweetness of a Savior who sacrifices so we could know Him and be close to Him in relationship?

THE GOAL OF BEING TRUTH-FILLED

Read Colossians 1:24–2:3.

Write verse 27 below.

What has God chosen to make known?

To what end had Paul struggled and worked to proclaim the truth?

Reread Colossians 2:2.

Below, record the things Paul said he desired/struggled for the believers in Colossae and Laodicea in verse 2.

Why do you think these things were so important for the early believers?

Do you think they are still important for believers today? Why or why not?

Paul was preoccupied with their encouragement in the truth. Encouragement here doesn't mean to simply feel motivated, blessed, or happy—he wasn't referring to a feeling but a state of being. The original word here for the word *encouragement* in the Greek means "to call alongside"—to be counseled, comforted, or strengthened.[5] In the Bible, the word *heart* often refers more closely to the mind, the epicenter of our whole persons.[6] If our actions follow our emotions, and our emotions follow what we believe is true, is it any wonder our hearts—or in the biblical equivalent, *minds*—must be encouraged?

Next, we'll practice encouraging our own hearts!

PRACTICE PREACHING TO YOUR OWN HEART

Charles Spurgeon warned against preaching a "Christless sermon":

> Sooner by far would I go to a bare table, and eat from a wooden
> porringer something that would appease my appetite, than
> I would go to a well-spread table on which there was nothing
> to eat. Yes, it is Christ, Christ, Christ whom we have to preach;
> and if we leave him out, we leave out the very soul of the
> gospel. Christless sermons make merriment for hell. Christless
> preachers, Christless Sunday-school teachers, Christless class-
> leaders, Christless tract-distributors,-what are all these doing?
> They are simply setting the mill to grind without putting any
> grist into the hopper, all their labor is in vain. If you leave
> Jesus Christ out, you are simply beating the air, or going to war
> without any weapon with which you can smite the foe.[7]

I don't know about you, but it's sobering to think on these words as I consider what I preach
to myself day by day.

What are some substitutions we tend to preach to ourselves and one another
instead of Christ alone?

Are you weary? Fearful? Lonely? Doubting? Burdened? Anxious? Longing for more? What your heart needs most is a clear reminder of who Christ is and what He's done for you.

Let's do just that—start reminding ourselves of who He is and what He has done and will do for us. As we learned in Session One, we're going to take one care that's on our minds and practice preaching the truth to ourselves about that specific issue. Just follow along with me below, reading the prompts and then filling in the chart on page 60.

> Why, my soul, are you downcast?
> Why so disturbed within me?
> Put your hope in God, for I will yet praise him,
> my Savior and my God.

PSALM 42:5, NIV

1 **Identify the care.** What's the issue? Why are you "downcast"?

2 **Tell your soul what to do.** Put your hope in God.

How do you put your hope in God? By recounting the hope of the gospel and the character of Christ: "Bless the LORD, O my soul, and forget not all his benefits" (Ps. 103:2). God's benefits are the ways He cares for us as His children, facts about His character, and what's true about Christ and our hope in Him.

3 **Embrace gospel hope.** How does the good news of Christ (the gospel) change your perspective?

Consider the reality that God is with you and for you in every moment, every struggle, every minute of unspoken despair, and even in days bursting with joy. He numbers your days with purpose and value, both now and eternally, and He's using your circumstances to make you look more like Jesus.

PREACHING TO YOUR OWN HEART

IDENTIFY THE CARE	TELL YOUR SOUL WHAT TO DO	EMBRACE GOSPEL HOPE
Write out your concern below.	Write out some of God's benefits.	Explain how gospel hope changes your perspective.

PRACTICE THE PATTERN

With Paul's example in mind, we're going to use the text of Colossians to preach the truth of the gospel to ourselves. Let's start off with the topic of peace, too often a scarce commodity in our hearts and minds.

I can have peace through Christ.

He made peace "by the blood of his cross" (Col. 1:20).

1 In what current circumstance do you feel a lack of peace—with others, with yourself, or with God?

2 Now, we're going to use the text of Colossians to craft a mini sermon to ourselves—to bring the truth of the gospel to bear in the part of your life that lacks peace. I've given you an example below, and then you'll have an opportunity to write your own.

Here's mine: Because Christ, in whom "all the fullness of God was pleased to dwell" (v. 19), offered Himself to pay the penalty for my rebellion toward God (v. 22), I don't need to try and find peace through pleasing God superficially or by pleasing others. Knowing Christ secured my peace with God allows me to approach my relationships with others and with God with humility and gratitude.

It's your turn! I know, dear friend, this can feel a little strange at first, but I promise it gets much easier as you get into the habit. You can do it! Keep at it.

3 Practice writing your own:

_____

_____

_____

_____

_____

You're doing great! OK, let's keep going by meditating on God's sovereignty.

God is sovereign.

He holds all things together (Col. 1:17).

1 In what current circumstance do you fight to control or manipulate?

You know the drill by now. We're going to use the text of Colossians to craft a mini sermon to ourselves—bring the truth of the gospel to bear in the part of your life that grasps for control and struggles to rest in God's loving and sovereign care. I've given you an example below, and then you'll have an opportunity to write your own.

2 Preach it to yourself:

Here's mine: Because Christ is the first, the beginning, and the One who rules, and He holds all things together (vv. 15-17), I don't need to be in charge all the time. I don't need to stress myself out trying to make sure everything happens perfectly and on time. The gospel saved me from that tyranny and promises me way better—God's timing and perfect plan.

3 Your turn again! Practice writing your own.

_____

_____

_____

_____

Close this week in prayer, thanking God for who He is and what He's done for us in Christ. Praise Him for perfect peace and total sovereignty.

SESSION THREE | SPRING

REHEARSE WHO YOU ARE

COLOSSIANS 2:4-23

66

Replacing lies with truth
is where this season begins.
Spring peeks out from the
long, dark days like a crocus
in new snowfall. Tender
growth knows the wind
and rain is yet to come,
so it clings to new roots,
anticipates the growth ahead,
and grounds itself in
what is right and true.

GRACELACED, SPRING[1]

Notes

#TRUTHFILLEDSTUDY

WELCOME

As we begin, discuss the following questions with your group:

Read Colossians 1:21-23 aloud in your group. According to this passage, why does Jesus reconcile believers to Himself? What does this tell you about God?

Discuss what it means to be holy, blameless, and beyond reproach as frail human beings.

As we learned in our study this week, encouragement has a deeper meaning than a feel-good pep talk. What is the biblical definition of encouragement? How does it change the way you might encourage your own heart (and others' hearts too)?

WATCH THE VIDEO

Feel free to use the space on the previous page to jot down notes as you watch Ruth's video teaching.

DISCUSS

Take a few moments to think through these questions from the video teaching or discuss them with your small group.

What comes to your mind when you think about God?

What's your favorite thing about God? Is something about Him hard for you to understand? Share it with a friend or your small group.

What would it look like practically for you to rest in the character of God instead of your circumstances? Give an example or two.

Take a few moments in prayer, asking God to help you trust Him and persevere in the winter seasons of the soul when it seems like nothing is happening. Thank Him for the work He is doing in your heart and mind, even if you can't see it. Consider friends who may especially be walking through a winter season of the heart. How might you encourage them to rest in God's character this week?

TO ACCESS THE VIDEO TEACHING SESSIONS,
USE THE INSTRUCTIONS IN THE BACK OF YOUR BIBLE STUDY BOOK.

69

I'm always giddy to see the first sign of crocus leaves poke through the winter's snow in the early spring. Their tiny green tips seem to proclaim and pronounce: "See! There's something growing here! All is not lost!" Not too long after the crocus' entrance, the snow begins to melt, and daffodils join in, followed by tulips—each vibrantly revealing how much work happens beneath the surface, long before blooms arrive.

It's not so different with seasons of the heart.

I imagine that our God's timing in how He orchestrates the first signs of life—in the midst of a bleak, long winter—is intentional and deliberate. If winter requires us to rest in the character of our God, spring calls us to rehearse the truths of what God says about who we are in Christ. You see, we rehearse the truth of our identity in Christ in spring seasons, when tender buds and new growth are happening, because young shoots need solid roots. There's no coming into bloom without being grounded in who God is and who He says we are in Him.

We started our study in the "winter" season of the heart because we can't trust what God says about us, His children, if we don't first trust what He says about Himself. As we learned last week, the apostle Paul followed a similar pattern as he reminded his readers of the wonders of the cross, the character of Christ, and all that Jesus accomplished on our behalf, before he instructed the believer in how to live in his or her true identity and to walk in faith. Remember, right believing leads to right living.

Why do we rehearse the truth?

We rehearse the truth of who we are because we so easily forget. Rehearsing is practice; it's repeating an action over and over again until it's second nature, until there's muscle memory.

I recently took a much needed break from social media and the internet in general. I was feeling over-saturated with information, anxious reading headlines, and lacking joy on account of being too entrenched in the online world and less present with the people right in front of me.

It proved to be one of the most fruitful and renewing decisions in this season, but it didn't happen naturally. Every day, for the first several days of committing to be off social media, I'd pick up my phone to check the time or to snap a photo, and my thumbs—my thumbs just did their own thing circling between apps in methodical order. It was automatic, involuntary, subconscious; it was like my left hand never got the memo about our Internet break.

Why would I struggle with mindlessly checking through apps? Muscle memory. I'd so rehearsed and practiced that motion over the years of working on my phone and being connected on social media that my body defaulted to what it was most familiar with.

What we practice and rehearse is what we will default to when storms threaten to crush the new buds forming in our lives. We must rehearse the truth of the gospel and our identity in Christ if we hope to default to truth and not lies.

PREACH THE TRUTH OF YOUR IDENTITY IN CHRIST

Read Colossians 2:4-23.

We are focusing this week on our identity in Christ—who He says we are in the light of who Jesus is.

Why is it so important to know who we are in Christ?

We can find the answer in the midst of Paul's purpose for writing Colossians. Let's look at Colossians 2:4-5:

> I say this in order that no one may delude you with plausible arguments. For though I am absent in body, yet I am with you in spirit, rejoicing to see your good order and the firmness of your faith in Christ.

That no one may delude you.

What voices try to delude you with plausible arguments?

I don't know about you, but sometimes that "no one" is me. I'm the one who deludes myself into thinking wrongly about my circumstances, about God's ways, about my purpose, about my future. In the same way that firmly grounded believers in Colossae could potentially find themselves duped or deluded by false teaching, we are equally at risk of falling for false messaging in our day.

The only way to combat wrong thinking is by filling our hearts and minds with truth. When we begin by resting in who God is, we can then rehearse the truth of who we are in Him. You recognize a counterfeit by knowing well the real thing.

I'm an ever-aspiring gardener. If you've ever planted flowers or vegetables, you know that all that fertilizing and watering nourishes the plants you intend to grow—and the weeds you didn't. How do you tell the difference? The only way to know the difference between a real flower or a weed is to study and know attributes and characteristics of the real thing. The weeds in our gardens will always try to crowd out and overwhelm the flowers we try to grow (just like the unruly lies that fill our minds!), so vigilance is key. We can't be casual about cultivation; we must know what we are feeding and growing. The more firmly grounded you are in what is true, the less likely you are to be uprooted and swayed, and the less likely you'll be to find your garden filled with lies rather than truth.

Now read how Paul talked about it in Colossians 2:6-7.

The apostle Paul first reminded the believers reading his letter how they were rooted and established in Christ. (You know how happy that makes this girl who loves all growing and planting metaphors and word pictures!)

The Bible often refers to roots and being firmly planted. Do you remember Psalm 1?

Turn to Psalm 1 in your Bible and read through the passage again.

What can we learn about being rooted and established in the Lord from this psalm?

THE BLESSED MAN **DOES NOT**	THE BLESSED MAN **DOES**

The blessed man who avoids what is false, counterfeit, and untrue, but chases the truth of God's Word "is like a _____ planted by _____ of water" (v. 3).

What happens to a plant when its roots are nourished and connected to the water source? It flourishes. It's fruitful. It prospers.

The psalmist wasn't referring to prosperity as we think of it: success, reward, ease. We clearly recognize that the righteous and deeply rooted believer is not always the one who prospers on earth or in tangible ways.

What do you think the psalmist meant?

Perhaps the psalm is referring to the prosperity of the soul—the fruitfulness that occurs for eternity when planted firmly on the soil of God's Word.

Reread Colossians 2:6.

"Therefore" in this verse points back to all the "riches of the glory . . . Christ in you, the hope of glory" (1:27) that He reminded us is ours as believers. What does that have to do with preaching to ourselves? When we are planted firmly in truth, we flourish and grow. When we flourish and grow, we are fruitful—producing a response. "Walk[ing] in him" (2:6) is the fruitful response that naturally overflows when we are nourished in the Word of God. (More about fruitful responses next session!)

Now, return to Colossians 2:7. It says,

> . . . rooted and built up in him and established in the faith, just as you were taught, abounding in thanksgiving.

How does being rooted, built up, and established in the faith lead you to abound in thanksgiving?

Paul painted a picture of growth here. He made it clear to his readers that as Christ-followers, our faith in Christ, through salvation, is how we are planted firmly and established in Him. To grow and be "built up," then, is a result of being nourished through the Word of God. The fruitfulness we see when a believer abounds in thanksgiving is evidence of the overflow of his or her heart. One can abound and be spiritually prosperous while lacking physical and monetary gain—some of the most thankful people live in the most humble circumstances. Every believer, regardless of his or her heritage, upbringing, biblical knowledge, or personal track record, can abound in thanksgiving if he or she is truly rooted in Christ through faith, abiding in Him.

According to Colossians 2:7, what are we supposed to rest in? And therefore, what can we rehearse? Meaning, what does this verse say about God? In light of that, what does this verse say about us?

Lord, thank You for Your Word and what it tells us about who we are because of Christ. Can You please help us to abide in You? Please teach us, by Your grace, how to be rooted and built up in our faith and how to rehearse who we are as we rest in the faithful character of God. In seasons of becoming, we gratefully depend on You. Amen.

KNOWING WHO YOU ARE IN CHRIST

Read Colossians 2:8-15.

Paul gave instruction here: "See to it that no one takes you captive by philosophy and empty deceit, according to human tradition, according to the elemental spirits of the world, and not according to Christ" (v. 8) and told the Colossians why they didn't need to fall for the deceptive teachings that were prevalent. They knew who they were in Christ!

You see, Paul's strategy for combatting falsehood was to be assured of truth—to rehearse our identity in Christ. Some of these concepts may be familiar to you, but it's OK if you're discovering these truths for the first time! Let's look at them together:

Reread Colossians 2:9-10.

What does it mean for the whole fullness of deity to dwell in Christ?

Jesus Christ is completely man and completely God. Jesus is God in human form. He lacks nothing and possesses all the power and divinity that God the Father possesses. Jesus is continually and forever one with God.

The phrase "you have been filled" (v. 10) speaks of a completed act with ongoing results. The fall in Genesis 3 made us by nature incomplete and broken, but at salvation, the believer—by faith in the redeeming work of Christ—becomes complete and a partaker "of the divine nature" (2 Pet. 1:4). By being filled with Christ, we share in the divine nature, power, and authority He has. We are filled in Him and therefore have everything we need in Him.

How does the fact that you have been filled in Christ, the Head of all rule and authority, encourage you in your life today?

Reread Colossians 2:11.

Circumcision was a required physical symbol for Jewish males, identifying them with their nationality and heritage. While it represented God's covenant with the Jewish people, the death and resurrection of Christ made the outward, physical symbol of "cutting off" no longer necessary in order to belong to God. Instead, through Jesus, we now spiritually "put off" our old sinful nature and are marked anew by our transformation in Christ.[2]

How does this significant symbol in Jewish culture and history reframe your understanding of how salvation changes your identity?

Reread Colossians 2:12.

Baptism is a picture—an outward display—of an inward reality. When believers truly trust in Christ for the forgiveness of their sins, they are dead to the enslavement of their former sinful nature (buried with Christ) and are alive (raised with Christ) and free in their new life in Christ. Believer's baptism declares that truth in a visible way.

How does this explanation of baptism help you properly consider who you were before Christ became your Savior and who you are after calling Him Lord?

Reread Colossians 2:13-14.

What can dead people do?

What position would uncircumcised Jews have?

Here, Paul reminded his readers that without Christ, no one is able to save themselves. No one is able to truly belong to God and be in His family. That was our condition before Jesus—helpless, inept, and without means to make things right.

But what did God do through Jesus?

"God _____ _____ together with him, having _____us all our trespasses, by _____ the record of debt that stood against us with its legal demands. This he _____ _____, nailing it to the cross" (vv. 13b-14).

That is the gospel! The good news of Jesus Christ in a nutshell!

Reread Colossians 2:15.

The death and resurrection of Christ defeated and disarmed Satan and his cohorts. God canceled our debt and brought us into the family of God when we were incapable of saving ourselves. His victory is how we can know with assurance who we are in Christ.

How does this truth reframe your confidence in your identity in Christ?

Now that we've unpacked these terms (are you not so encouraged when you see these truths one by one?), rewrite each one in your own words: *What does it mean that you are circumcised with Christ? What reality do we declare as those whose sinful nature is buried with Christ and raised to new life?* These are the truths we will need to preach to ourselves when the philosophies and empty deceits of our day try to take us captive.

What is true about you?

YOU HAVE BEEN FILLED IN HIM,	
CIRCUMCISED . . . BY THE CIRCUMCISION OF CHRIST,	
BURIED WITH HIM IN BAPTISM,	
RAISED WITH HIM THROUGH FAITH,	
WERE DEAD IN TRESPASSES,	
MADE ALIVE TOGETHER WITH HIM,	
FORGIVEN OF YOUR TRESPASSES.	

This, friends, is our testimony if we are in Christ. Who we were. What Christ has done. Who we are because of the blood of Christ. Paul could've easily said: *Hey friends, you're doing great as believers. Keep up the good work and have faith!* But he didn't. He took the time to lay out where they'd been, how far they'd come, and how the gospel changes everything.

It is easy to be duped, confused, or taken "captive by philosophy and empty deceit" (v. 8) when we are not rooted and grounded in truth. And the truth of God's Word—and the story it tells of God redeeming His people—is complete with a beginning, middle, and end. It's a full picture of how sin wrecked our fellowship with God, how Christ came to pay the price to restore that fellowship, and how we are changed and made new when we die to our sinful past and live to a sanctified life.

Be detailed and write your own story or testimony. I've provided a few prompts to get you started.

Where were you before Christ?

What did Jesus do to cause you to belong to Him?

Who are you now in Christ?

Finally, read Colossians 2:16-23.

The false teachings in Colossae insisted on legalism, asceticism, and self-denial as a means to gain spiritual enlightenment. Legalism teaches an achievement or works-based way to God. The false teachers of Paul's day were trying to convince the Colossians that it wasn't enough to put their faith in Jesus; they needed to keep the Law, even in regard to food and drink. While God gave the Law to the Jewish people as a way to distinguish them and set them apart from other nations, the Bible tells us that Jesus came to make a new way—a new covenant—that replaces outward rules with inward change. Legalism relies on man's effort, but redemption relies on God's.

Similarly, asceticism placed hope in self-denial and harsh treatment of the body as a means to please God. The church in Paul's day was fed a lie that the body was evil and one could be free by denying it. While those who subscribed to asceticism and self-denial appeared holy or religious, Paul's point was that it was actually vain and self-centered—making more of human effort than dependence on the grace and mercy of God. You see, it doesn't matter how holy and sacrificial you look with your actions, service, or outward humility. If you are trusting in those things to make you worthy to a holy God, you're worshiping a self-made religion—it's not the gospel.

Paul said these things have "an appearance of wisdom in promoting self-made religion" (v. 23) but have no true power for godly living.

> What are some current, personal examples of legalism, false humility, or self-made religion that might appear to be spiritual or holy but are really dangerous lies that promote your own effort rather than Christ's finished work?

Here's what I'd share if we were having coffee: I see my tendency toward legalism when I pride myself on having consistent time in the Word or condemn myself when I'm not. I see my own propensity toward self-made religion when I'm tempted to manage my walk with the Lord through some formula of dos and don'ts, thinking holiness can somehow be achieved in any means other than through dependence on Jesus.

> How does knowing who you are in Christ help you combat false ideas and lies about the Christian life?

PRACTICE PREACHING TO YOUR OWN HEART

> Why, my soul, are you downcast?
> Why so disturbed within me?
> Put your hope in God, for I will yet praise him,
> my Savior and my God.

PSALM 42:5, NIV

1 **Identify the care.** What's the issue? Why are you "downcast"?

2 **Tell your soul what to do.** Put your hope in God.

How do you put your hope in God? By recounting the hope of the gospel and the character of Christ: "Bless the LORD, O my soul, and forget not all his benefits" (Ps. 103:2). God's benefits are the ways He cares for us as His children, facts about His character, and what's true about Christ and our hope in Him.

3 **Embrace gospel hope.** How does the good news of Christ (the gospel) change your perspective?

Consider the reality that God is with you and for you in every moment, every struggle, every moment of unspoken despair, and even in days bursting with joy. He numbers your days with purpose and value, both now and eternally, and He's using your circumstances to make you look more like Jesus.

PREACHING TO YOUR OWN HEART

IDENTIFY THE CARE

Write out your
concern below.

TELL YOUR SOUL WHAT TO DO

Write out some of
God's benefits.

EMBRACE GOSPEL HOPE

Explain how
gospel hope changes
your perspective.

PRACTICE THE PATTERN

I am forgiven.

I am forgiven of all of my trespasses in Christ.

1. In what current circumstance do you feel guilt or shame, forgetting the price paid for your sin?

2. Preach it to yourself:

   Here's mine: Because the blood of Christ paid the penalty for my sin, "canceling the record of debt that stood against us with its legal demands" (Col. 2:14), God no longer looks at me as a guilty debtor, but as forgiven. I don't need to keep punishing myself for my failures and my sinful choices in the past; I can receive the gift of a debt paid in full.

3. Practice writing your own:

   _____

   _____

   _____

   _____

I am raised with Him.

Because Jesus rose again, I, too, am raised through faith from spiritual death.

1 In what current circumstance do you long to see victory?

2 Preach it to yourself:

Here's mine: Because Jesus did not stay buried in death, but was raised to life, I—through baptism—am symbolically buried in death to my old way of living and am raised to new life in Christ. I no longer need to try and clean myself up or use legalistic means to claim victory over habits and sinful patterns; I can trust the saving work of Christ to put to death my sin and lift me out of it through faith in Jesus.

3 Practice writing your own:

SESSION FOUR | SUMMER

RESPOND IN FAITH

COLOSSIANS 3:1-4:1

92

The fruit
of summer
sweetly proves
the roots that
deepen beneath
in other seasons.

GRACELACED, SUMMER[1]

Notes

group time

WELCOME

As we begin, discuss the following questions with your group:

This week in our discussion of who we are in Christ, which attribute or description resonated with you the most? Why?

How does being rooted in the truth of Christ lead to thanksgiving?

As we read in Colossians, no one can save herself. We all need Christ to be ushered into the family of God and to walk in a way that pleases Him. Does this realization bring you comfort? Stress? Explain.

WATCH THE VIDEO

Feel free to use the space on the previous page to jot down notes as you watch Ruth's video teaching.

DISCUSS

Take a few moments to think through these questions from the video teaching or discuss them with your small group.

Do you sometimes struggle to remember who you are in Christ? Do certain circumstances or relationships make it tougher? Explain.

As we discussed in our video time together, the words that we say over and over again to ourselves about who we are become significant. Consider: what life-giving messages are you telling yourself? Condemning messages?

Take a few moments to write down your story of redemption—how you came to know Christ—or refer back to your answers on page 82. If you feel comfortable, share it with your small group.

Find one or two truth-filled messages from God's Word that you plan to rehearse this week to help you grow well-watered, deeply-set roots. Make it a point to think on them throughout the week.

TO ACCESS THE VIDEO TEACHING SESSIONS,
USE THE INSTRUCTIONS IN THE BACK OF YOUR BIBLE STUDY BOOK.

95

When I think about the seasons of a believer's life in Christ, I think of summer as the season of fruitful service and obedience. It's the season we all run toward—like the actual season filled with ripe strawberries, pool parties, lush vegetable gardens, and long days of playing out in the sun.

Summer's season of the heart is when fruit is measurable, abundance is tangible, and what's true inside is made visible by what appears on the outside. And just as a garden yields much fruit in response to well-nourished growth, our offerings of service and obedience can only extend from the foundation of where we've been thus far in the study: resting in the character of God and rehearsing the truth of who we are in Him.

Like we talked about the first week, sometimes this is the season we long to run to as believers—to shortcut the other seasons and go straight to the one that shows off fruit, helps us feel productive, and satisfies our desire to do, rather than simply be.

Who doesn't love blooms? Fruit? Results?

But the practice of preaching truth to ourselves is not a fast-fix formula. It's not meant to simply help us appear fruitful and truth-filled; it's meant to establish us deeply in the Word that we might overflow in good works.

WHY DO WE RESPOND IN FAITH?

Have you ever bought a gift out of obligation or guilt? You know the feeling—trying to pick out a gift for someone, striving to be liked, approved, or hoping your gift meets expectations. Oh, what a nerve-racking way to offer a gift!

That's how it is when we try to act faithfully apart from believing rightly about the gifts we offer, why we offer them, and the recipient of our faithfulness.

But how different it is when you're choosing a present for someone you know loves you deeply, who welcomes you, fights for you, sacrifices for you, whose love for you doesn't change even if you're having a bad day. When we're motivated to give by love, what we give and the way we do so changes.

Our *why* changes our response and our *how*.

This is why—besides being a lover of seasons!—I'm walking us through the practice of preaching truth to ourselves, starting with what we believe about God (winter), followed by what we believe He says about us (spring), and now with what we do in response (summer).

I don't know about you, but sometimes I am eager to see fruit in my life but forgetful about how that fruit is actually produced.

Read the familiar passage about fruit in Galatians 5:16-25, especially taking note of verses 16 and 22-24:

But I say, walk by the Spirit, and you will not gratify the desires of the flesh (v. 16).

But the fruit of the Spirit is love, joy, peace, patience, kindness, goodness, faithfulness, gentleness, self-control; against such things there is no law. And those who belong to Christ Jesus have crucified the flesh with its passions and desires (vv. 22-24).

What did Paul mean by "walk by the Spirit"? How is it synonymous with "led by the Spirit" in verse 18?

These verses help explain the *how* of the passage in Colossians we read last session. In Colossians 2:6 Paul challenged believers to walk in Christ. In what ways does Galatians 5:16-25 help direct our steps?

What are the "works of the flesh" (vv. 19-21)?

Why do you think Paul described the evidence of being led by the flesh as "works" but the evidence of being led by the Spirit as "fruit"?

Describe a time when you tried to obey apart from a response to God's grace and your faith in His work of redemption.

Did it feel like work or fruit?

If fruit is born of abiding and work is born of striving, we bear the fruit of obedience when we remain (abide) in the truth of God's character and what He's accomplished through the gospel and whom He's made us to be as a result. Now, let's look at what we preach to ourselves in the summer.

CHOOSING TO OBEY WITH YOUR MIND

Read Colossians 3:2.

In the first two chapters of Colossians, Paul established the foundation of the Colossians' faith. He made it clear Christ gave the believers in Colossae new life, and they could stand fast in their identity in Him.

Colossians 3:2 says, "Set your minds on things that are above, not on things that are on earth." Isn't this the very thing we're talking about here in this study? To set our minds on truth, not worldly wisdom. To be filled with the treasure of eternal things, not earthly things. To keep steadily fixed upon the Word of God, not the opinions of other people.

A familiar sister passage, also from Paul, is Philippians 4:8.

> Finally brothers and sisters, whatever is true, whatever is honorable, whatever is just, whatever is pure, whatever is lovely, whatever is commendable—if there is any moral excellence and if there is anything praiseworthy—dwell on these things (CSB).

What can we conclude about what we are to think and dwell on based upon Paul's instruction in both letters?

With words like *fix*, *dwell*, and *think upon* (in other translations), name a few adjectives that describe what Paul was getting at.

If you used words like *intentional, steadfast,* and *unshaken,* you're on the right track. Both words in the original Greek from both verses are in the present imperative meaning: *Follow this command habitually and continually, making it a way of life day by day.*[2, 3]

"Set your mind"; "dwell on these things" in response to, in faith, the truth of God's Word.

Describe some concrete ways you can make this a practice in your life this week. How can you remind yourself of the truth of God's Word and practice dwelling in what is true?

PREACH THE TRUTH OF "PUTTING ON"

Read Colossians 3:1–4:1.

Paul began to tell the Colossians and us how to respond in the light of these truths. He started in verse one with the phrase, "If then you have been raised with Christ." All the instructions that follow for the Christ-follower are predicated on his or her position as a co-heir, buried and raised with Christ.

Below, list the instructions that immediately follow the truths of our identity in Christ.

1. Seek _____

2. Put to death _____

3. Put away _____

4. Do not _____

5. Put on _____

6. Let the peace of Christ _____

7. Let the word of Christ _____

8. Whatever you do _____

9. Give thanks _____

Wow! That's quite an intense picture of the Christian life, right? Do you see how if we jumped straight to this list—this chapter of Colossians—without being filled with the truth of the first three sessions, we'd be tempted to "put on" these acts of faith without being rooted in the truth that enables us to respond this way in the first place?

What would be the result of trying to "put on" these acts of faith without being rooted in the truth found in the first two chapters of Colossians?

How have you seen that kind of behavior in your life or in the lives of those around you?

Our response in faith has an order. We must put off the old self before we can put on the new self. Which is to say, to respond in obedience and faith to God's work in our lives is to respond in denying and putting to death what previously ruled our hearts—our sinful, self-focused thoughts.

This is why we preach truth to ourselves.

Any form of obedience, fruitfulness, and faithfulness is a work of the Spirit in the life of a believer who is grounded in the truth of his or her salvation and the redeeming work of Christ. Our response in faith is a love offering of gratitude as we receive the gift of God's grace.

Preach it to yourself:

God doesn't desire for you to work at looking the part of a holy Christian; He longs for you to abide in Him so He might faithfully bring about fruit in your life.

KNOWING HOW TO HONOR HIM IN OUR RELATIONSHIPS

Paul finished this section of his letter with household instructions for the believer. These exhortations were meant to free, not bind. They were meant to be a means of showing off the great grace of God in the transformed lives of a believer. Sometimes we're tempted to think that our messy relationship struggles are modern, but Paul knew these relationships as difficult, costly, and challenging to the believer and non-believer alike, even in the first century. However, he also knew these relationships were an opportunity for Christ-followers to live and respond differently than non-believers to the issues in their everyday lives.

For the sake of this study and our focus on the practice of preaching truth to ourselves, I want to encourage us to look at the instructions Paul gave in the light of putting on the new self in Christ (v. 10) and the exhortation to "put on love, which binds everything together in perfect harmony . . . [letting] the peace of Christ rule in your hearts, to which indeed you were called in one body" (vv. 14-15).

Wives and Husbands

How does putting on love and letting the peace of Christ rule their hearts cause wives to respond in humility and submission?

How does putting on love and letting the peace of Christ rule their hearts cause husbands to respond sacrificially and respectfully?

Children and Parents

How does putting on love and letting the peace of Christ rule their hearts cause children to respond with honor and reverence?

How does putting on love and letting the peace of Christ rule their hearts cause parents to respond with encouragement and responsibility?

Employee and Employers

In Paul's day, the relationship of master and slave ranged between true servitude to hired hand. Though inadequate as a parallel, a modern-day context we can give to the historical slave/master motif in Scripture is that of employer and employee. The point of the instruction here is to encourage Christ-honoring behavior when subject to authority. Paul admonished believers to pursue godliness with sincerity on account of our true authority being God Himself.

How does putting on love and letting the peace of Christ rule their hearts cause employees to respond with diligence and accountability to the Lord?

How does putting on love and letting the peace of Christ rule their hearts cause employers to respond with equity and accountability to the Lord?

THE FUEL FOR OUR CONTINUAL RESPONSE OF OBEDIENCE

I want to close this week's study in drawing our attention to one of my favorite verses in Scripture, a verse that summarizes the entire intent of this study: Be steeped in the Word; encourage one another in it, and let thanksgiving drive you to perseverance.

> Let the word of Christ dwell in you richly, teaching
> and admonishing one another in all wisdom,
> singing psalms and hymns and spiritual songs, with
> thankfulness in your hearts to God.
>
> COLOSSIANS 3:16

This is the very reason we are studying the practice of preaching truth to ourselves. This practice is not self-betterment, a strategy for greater productivity, or a way to positive thinking. It's realignment with the reason for our obedience and the fuel that drives it.

Lord, will You help us to know the true why behind our obedience? Sometimes we are so busy going through the motions that we forget to root our doing in a love for You. Please remind us of who You are and how You love us. As we set our minds on things above and preach the truth to ourselves, we ask for Your Spirit to enable our fruit, faith, perseverance, and gratitude. Amen.

PRACTICE PREACHING TO YOUR OWN HEART

> Why, my soul, are you downcast?
> Why so disturbed within me?
> Put your hope in God, for I will yet praise him,
> my Savior and my God.

PSALM 42:5, NIV

1   **Identify the care.** What's the issue? Why are you "downcast"?

2   **Tell your soul what to do.** Put your hope in God.

How do you put your hope in God? By recounting the hope of the gospel and the character of Christ: "Bless the LORD, O my soul, and forget not all his benefits" (Ps. 103:2). God's benefits are the ways He cares for us as His children, facts about His character, and what's true about Christ and our hope in Him.

3   **Embrace gospel hope.** How does the good news of Christ (the gospel) change your perspective?

Consider the reality that God is with you and for you in every moment, every struggle, every moment of unspoken despair, and even in days bursting with joy. He numbers your days with purpose and value, both now and eternally, and He's using your circumstances to make you look more like Jesus.

PREACHING TO YOUR OWN HEART

IDENTIFY THE CARE	TELL YOUR SOUL WHAT TO DO	EMBRACE GOSPEL HOPE
Write out your concern below.	Write out some of God's benefits.	Explain how gospel hope changes your perspective.

PRACTICE THE PATTERN

God tells me to put off slander.

It does not honor the Lord when I speak ill of others (v. 8).

1 In what current relationship do you try to maneuver or manipulate, forgetting that you've died to the old ways of making yourself great and others less than?

2 Preach it to yourself:

Here's mine: Because I've been buried with Christ, I can put off slander and any form of self-promotion that once made me feel better about myself. My worth is not in being the best or making someone else out to be the worst. I can respond in obedience with the words I speak about others because I belong to Jesus.

3 Practice writing your own:

_____

_____

_____

God tells me to work heartily.

Work diligently for the Lord and not for approval of others (v. 23).

1 In what current situation do you need to bring your best—for the Lord's sake—not for others to like you?

2 Preach it to yourself:

Here's mine: Because I get to put the gospel on display in the way I work, follow through, or do what I say I will do, I can work diligently even when no one is applauding me because I no longer need to please others (v. 22) but only the Lord Himself.

3 Practice writing your own:

WE DO NOT KNOW WHAT TO DO, BUT *our eyes are on You*

2 CHRONICLES 20:17

SESSION FIVE | FALL

REMEMBER GOD'S PROVISION

COLOSSIANS 4:2-18

116

Just as fields slow down and quiet themselves, so we embrace Fall's changes, knowing Who supplies all things when the blooming season comes to an end.

GRACELACED, FALL[1]

117

Notes

WELCOME

As we begin, discuss the following questions with your group:

What does it mean to "walk by the Spirit" (Gal. 5:16)?

Share your ideas from this week's study—practical ways you can remind yourself of God's Word and help yourself dwell on what is true.

What would it look like for you to "let the peace of Christ rule in your hearts" (Col. 3:15) this week? Share with your group any difficult circumstances or situations that might try to rob you of your peace so they can pray for you and encourage you toward peace in God.

WATCH THE VIDEO

Feel free to use the space on the previous page to jot down notes as you watch Ruth's video teaching.

DISCUSS

Take a few moments to think through these questions from the video teaching or discuss them with your small group.

Are you sometimes hesitant to read the entirety of Scripture? Do you find it easier to focus on only your favorite verses or inspirational thoughts? Why is it important to read Bible passages in their larger contexts?

Most of the time, do you obey God out of love for Him? Or some other motive like the fear of rejection or a need to prove yourself? Explain.

When you consider the practice of "putting on" habits that honor God and "putting off" habits that dishonor Him, do you have any reservations? Fears? Concerns? Share them with your group or a friend.

Close your time together in prayer, asking God to continue to teach you more about His loving-kindness and to help you obey out of love and not obligation.

I've never been a terribly successful gardener, at least not in a way that causes our family to eat from our home grown produce instead of the grocery store. My husband Troy once joked, after we spent hundreds of dollars on watering my potager through a sweltering New Mexico summer, that my meager veggies were some of the most expensive organic produce we've ever eaten.

But I know enough about gardening to know that fruitful gardens do not stay neat and tidy. They explode and expand. Those perfect rows become overgrown; the vines take over; and occasionally fruit gets overlooked and collects on the soil below. Growth looks messy. Growth stretches all the resources. Growth takes work. And growth makes weariness worth it.

A fruitful garden that yields a bounty is often the most spent and unsightly at the end of the season. When fall arrives and all the overgrown zucchini have been harvested, hidden cucumbers extracted, and pumpkins picked through, what remains are unwieldy vines and withered foliage. In the same way that a garden explodes and then must recoup after being spent, fall is a season of the heart that reestablishes and reminds a believer where his or her provision for perseverance comes from.

WHY WE MUST REMEMBER GOD'S PROVISION

As much as we all love a season of great growth, it can be tempting to forget—in the midst of fruitfulness—that our fruit bearing isn't sustainable without God's faithfulness to keep us, hold us fast, and provide for our continued progress.

Good watering habits, disciplined pruning, and well-kept garden beds alone won't cause us to be fruitful in gardening or in our spiritual lives. If we forgetfully take credit for our own resourcefulness or ability to produce beautiful byproducts of faith, we'll inevitably take on a burden we were never meant to carry. God is the author and finisher of our faith. Especially in a weary and worn season of fall, we must remember "it is God who works in you, both to will and to work for his good pleasure" (Phil. 2:13). Otherwise, we can be equally tempted to give ourselves too much credit for the fruitful work we see or become fearfully doubtful that we can continue in a path of fruitfulness. Neither are helpful responses, and neither are grounded in truth.

So this week we will focus on remembering God's provision in the fall season of the heart.

Read Philippians 1:6 below.

> And I am sure of this, that he who began a good
> work in you will bring it to completion at the day of
> Jesus Christ.

Why do you think Paul wrote this familiar reminder to his reader?

Describe the conditions and circumstances in which you are prone to feel the most incapable of persevering.

What are some ways you try to sustain your own fruitfulness or secure your own progress?

How can you tell the difference between striving in your own strength and trusting God to bring His work into completion?

Read Philippians 2:12-13 below.

Therefore, my beloved, as you have always obeyed, so now, not only as in my presence but much more in my absence, work out your own salvation with fear and trembling, for it is God who works in you, both to will and to work for his good pleasure.

What do you notice about God's part and your part in Paul's instruction to the Philippians?

GOD'S PART	YOUR PART

The original form of "work out" in this passage indicates a progressive, continual outworking of the action.[2] Because the work of sanctification happens from the moment we are saved until the moment we are with Jesus in eternity, the idea here is that believers must continue to take seriously the consequences of sin, the hope of redemption, and the truth of our identity in Christ. Formation in the Christian life doesn't happen overnight; it is a process through which God does the transforming while we respond to Him through His Word.

What do you think Paul meant by the phrase "with fear and trembling"? What does that indicate about our part of diligence and growth in our faith?

How do we work out our salvation? Be as specific as you can.

PREACH THE TRUTH ABOUT HOLDING FAST

If anyone was weary and worn, it would've been the apostle Paul. He was writing this letter to the Colossians from prison, remember? His example and instruction at the close of this letter is our example for steadfastness.

Read Colossians 4:2-6.

Paul closed his letter to the Colossians with a reminder to stand firm and be watchful. The phrase "continue steadfastly" or in some translations "devote yourselves" (v. 2) is derived from a Greek word meaning to endure, be courageously persistent, to be steadfast, to persevere.[3]

What are the three parts of Paul's exhortation here—the three things he asked the Colossians to do?

1.

2.

3.

Paul preached to the Colossians so they could remember where their help comes from.

How does continuing steadfastly in prayer with thanksgiving look different from the way you are currently praying to the Lord? No one will see your answer—think about it and answer honestly.

Paul penned this letter for encouragement and instruction—beginning with what the Colossians had in Christ, followed by who they were as followers of Jesus, and then how they were to live in response to faith in Christ. (Look back through the last four weeks at where we've been!) Paul's final instruction to the Colossians was to be intentional with the way they used their speech and how they lived out the words they said they believed:

> Walk in wisdom toward outsiders, making the best use of the time. Let your speech always be gracious, seasoned with salt, so that you may know how you ought to answer each person (vv. 5-6).

What does it mean to have gracious speech, "seasoned with salt"?

How does preaching the gospel to yourself overflow to your speech with other people?

The last four sessions have been about preaching words of gospel truth and hope to ourselves, just as Paul instructed the Colossians to remember the truths for themselves. Paul seems to end his letter as if to say: "Keep speaking the gospel and live out what you say you believe!"

And so it is with the practice of preaching truth to ourselves. We are to: "Keep speaking the gospel to ourselves and live out what we say we believe!"

Preaching the truth of the gospel to ourselves is to agree with Jesus: He is the Savior; He is the Provider; He is faithful.

Read Colossians 4:7-18.

This final section of Colossians may not prescriptively show us what to preach to ourselves, but it sets an example of how we remember God's provision.

What are the words Paul used to describe each fellow ministry partner?

Tychicus	
Onemsimus	
Aristarchus, Mark, and Justus	
Epaphras	
Luke and Demas	

How does acknowledging God's faithfulness in others encourage your own heart?

Paul, in chains, sought to encourage his brothers and sisters in Christ by reminding them of how God provided for him and how God provided for them, the recipients of the letter. God's provision doesn't always change our circumstances (Paul was still writing from prison!), but it does change the way we see our circumstances.

Whom has God provided in your life to encourage you in faithfulness?

Who in your life could use encouragement right now? Make a plan to send them a quick note or text this week doing just that!

Lord, we thank You for every season of the soul, the bountiful seasons bursting with fruit and the seasons when the land lies fallow in rest. In seasons when You ask us to walk by faith because we can't see where You are working, please remind us that You hold on to us with Your love.
We trust Your heart as You care for us. With You, no season is wasted. We're grateful for the ministry partners You've given to point us to Your goodness and faithfulness. May we do the same for those around us, to Your honor and glory. Amen.

PREACH THE TRUTH OF HIS CARE

Psalm 23 is one of the best known passages in Scripture that reminds us of God's faithfulness. It's familiar, and sometimes we treat it like beautiful poetry but forget it's a powerful reminder and declaration of God's provision.

Read Psalm 23 slowly and jot down in your own words what David described as God's provision in the metaphor of a shepherd.

"The Lᴏʀᴅ is my shepherd; I shall not want" (v. 1).

"He makes me lie down in green pastures" (v. 2).

"He leads me beside still waters" (v. 2).

"He restores my soul" (v. 3).

"He leads me in paths of righteousness for his name's sake" (v. 3).

"Even though I walk through the valley of the shadow of death, I will fear no evil, for you are with me; your rod and your staff, they comfort me" (v. 4).

"You prepare a table before me in the presence of my enemies" (v. 5);

"You anoint my head with oil; my cup overflows" (v. 5).

"Surely goodness and mercy shall follow me all the days of my life" (v. 6),

"and I shall dwell in the house of the LORD forever" (v. 6).

Humor me: If sheep could speak, what are some things they might say to themselves or to one another when their shepherd is not near?

What, instead, would a sheep speak under the care of its shepherd?

PRACTICE THE PATTERN

I have what I need.

God's provision is always complete.

1 In what area of your life are you tempted to doubt that God will meet your needs? Where do you feel you're lacking?

2 Preach it to yourself:

> And my God will supply all your needs according to his riches in glory in Christ Jesus.
>
> PHILIPPIANS 4:19, CSB

> Every good gift and every perfect gift is from above, coming down from the Father of lights, with whom there is no variation or shadow due to change.
>
> JAMES 1:17

What are His riches in glory in Christ Jesus?

See Ephesians 3:16-19.

3 Practice writing your own:

Because God's provision is always complete, I can . . .

_____

_____

_____

I am well cared for by God.

God's provision is always effective.

1 Do you ever see what God has given and doubt that it's best? In what relationship or part of your life? Explain.

2 Preach it to yourself:

> . . . seeing that His divine power has granted to us everything pertaining to life and godliness, through the true knowledge of Him who called us by His own glory and excellence.
>
> 2 PETER 1:3, NASB

How does the knowledge of Him give you practical ways to pursue godliness today?

③ Practice writing your own:

Because God's provision is always effective right now, I can . . .

_____

_____

_____

I am secure in Christ because of the gospel.
God's provision is always ultimately through the gospel.

① Do you ever try to earn God's favor and provision? Why do you think you can be good enough to merit His help?

② Preach it to yourself:

> Truly my soul finds rest in God; my salvation comes from him.
>
> PSALM 62:1, NIV

> I will refresh the weary and satisfy the faint.
>
> JEREMIAH 31:25, NIV

Look at the birds of the air, that they do not sow, nor reap nor gather into barns, and yet your heavenly Father feeds them. Are you not worth much more than they?

MATTHEW 6:26, NASB

Come to Me, all who are weary and heavy-laden, and I will give you rest.

MATTHEW 11:28, NASB

3 Practice writing your own:

Because God's provision is always ultimately through the gospel, I can . . .

Rock of Ages, Cleft for me
Let me hide myself in Thee.

You make known to me the path of life in Your presence there is fullness of joy at Your right hand are pleasures forevermore.

PSALM 16:11

SESSION SIX | PUT IT INTO PRACTICE

PUT IT
INTO
PRACTICE

140

Let us hold fast the confession of our hope without wavering, for he who promised is faithful.

HEBREWS 10:23

Notes

WELCOME

As we begin, discuss the following questions with your group:

What does it mean to "work out your own salvation" (Phil. 2:12)? How do you work it out in your everyday lives?

God's provision doesn't always change our circumstances, but it does change the way we see our circumstances. How have you seen this be true in your own life?

Remembering our study of Psalm 23 this week, what would a sheep say under the care of a good and faithful shepherd? Share your answer with the group.

WATCH THE VIDEO

Feel free to use the space on the previous page to jot down notes as you watch Ruth's video teaching.

DISCUSS

Take a few moments to think through these questions from the video teaching or discuss them with your small group.

In our video time together, we discussed the need for seasons of rest and recovery. How do you normally welcome seasons of rest? Do you struggle to be still? Explain.

How have you seen God provide for you recently? Share how He has shown Himself faithful to you.

What makes an encouraging person? Name a few actions or attributes that encourage you.

In closing, take some time to tell your small group about a Tychicus in your life, a person who consistently points you toward God and encourages you to keep pressing forward even when things are hard. (Maybe you have a friend like that in your small group?)

TO ACCESS THE VIDEO TEACHING SESSIONS,
USE THE INSTRUCTIONS IN THE BACK OF YOUR BIBLE STUDY BOOK.

143

TRUTHFILLED

Seasons of the heart are just that—seasons. We grow accustomed to the changing seasons in the natural world, but when it comes to walking with Jesus, we're often surprised when we have seasons of painful waiting and unrest—pushing us to find our rest in the character of the God we serve. Or sometimes we find ourselves in a season of new growth—where our identity in Christ is discovered anew, forging new paths of growth and maturity in our lives. And some seasons prove incredibly full as we reap the fruit of obedience and respond in faith. And finally, just as the growing season looks different in the fall, sometimes we must call upon reminders of God's provision when we are weary and spent.

The practice of preaching truth to yourself is not a magic pill or a formula for guaranteed results. My prayer is that through this study, you've seen the Bible is the story of God's pursuit of us—and is a book full of truths meant to change the way we think, believe, feel, and live. The emphasis is on the word "practice." It takes time, and it takes repetitively applying the gospel to every situation, day by day, moment by moment. The gospel doesn't simply apply to everything because it gives answers and solutions to individual concerns, but because when we remember the truths of who God is, who we are in Christ, how we can respond in faith, and how the Lord provides for our perseverance—everything changes.

We've practiced the content and pattern of preaching truth to ourselves through the Book of Colossians. In this final week of our study, we will practice what we've learned with additional passages of Scripture. You will find that, as you begin reading the Bible with the desire to preach truth to your own heart, the application of those truths will become easier for you to mine from the riches of His Word.

REST IN HIS CHARACTER

Read Psalm 27.

Look for what this passage says about who God is: His attributes, His heart, His purposes, His plan of salvation. Record what you find.

Who is God, and why is He trustworthy?

Who is Jesus, and how has He saved us?

Write a sermon for your own heart:

REHEARSE YOUR IDENTITY IN CHRIST

Read Ephesians 1.

Look for what this passage says about who you are in Christ: your inheritance, your new identity, your nature, your redemption. Write your findings below.

How are you a new creation in Christ?

How does God see you in contrast to how you view yourself?

Write a sermon for your own heart:

RESPOND IN FAITH

Read Hebrews 10:19-27.

Look for what this passage says about how we can respond in faith and
obedience to Jesus: God's empowerment, your response, fruit of obedience,
faith's work in you. Jot down your notes below.

How does God want you to respond to what you know to be true?

What can you do in faith today because you trust Christ and believe what
God says is true about you?

Write a sermon for your own heart:

REMEMBER HIS PROVISION

Read Matthew 6:25-34.

Look for what this passage says about how God provides for us: our physical needs, our emotional needs, our spiritual needs, our perseverance. Below, note what you find.

How does God sustain you?

How is God faithful in providing in big and small ways for all your seen and unseen needs?

Write a sermon for your own heart:

Lord, teach us to replace the noisy concerns in our minds and hearts with confidence in Your holy Word. Help us to truly rest in Your faithfulness, sovereignty, goodness, and unfailing love for us. Show us our purpose when we rehearse who we are in Christ, our new identity. When we've anchored ourselves in You and who You've made us to become in Christ, lead us to respond in faith and obedience as children of God. And when we grow weary, help us to remember that You alone provide. Thank You for the rich blessing of Your Word and the transformation it brings through the Spirit's work in us. May the gospel change everything as we continue to practice preaching truth to ourselves. Amen.

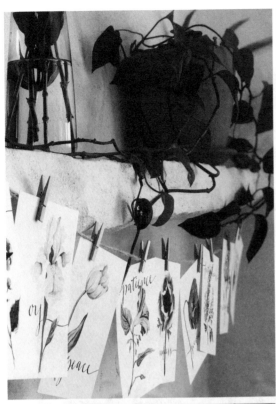

SESSION SEVEN | COMMISSIONING

COMMISSIONING

154

...walk in a manner worthy of the Lord, fully pleasing to him: bearing fruit in every good work and increasing in the knowledge of God...

COLOSSIANS 1:10

Notes

group time

WELCOME

As we begin, discuss the following questions with your group:

With Psalm 27 in mind, discuss the trustworthiness of God.

With Ephesians 1 in mind, unpack the way God sees you in contrast to the faulty way you sometimes see yourself.

With Hebrews 10:19-27 in mind, how can you respond in faith and obedience to Jesus?

With Matthew 6:25-34 in mind, detail some of the many ways God sustains you.

WATCH THE VIDEO

Feel free to use the space on the previous page to jot down notes as you watch Ruth's video teaching.

DISCUSS

Take a few moments to think through these questions from the video teaching or discuss them with your small group.

Read Romans 12:2 together. After six weeks in Bible study, how do you now view the practice of preaching truth to yourself and renewing your mind with God's Word?

As you have been intentional to fill your heart and mind with truth, have you noticed a difference in the way you feel and act? Are your feelings and actions more in line with God's purposes than they used to be?

Name one truth or takeaway that you've learned from our six weeks together. Why does it resonate with you so much?

Take a few moments to celebrate, thanking God for His truth and the promise His Word holds for His children.

TO ACCESS THE VIDEO TEACHING SESSIONS,
USE THE INSTRUCTIONS IN THE BACK OF YOUR BIBLE STUDY BOOK.

ENDNOTES

LETTER FROM THE AUTHOR

1. Ruth Chou Simons, *Gracelaced: Discover Timeless Truths Through Seasons of the Heart* (Eugene, OR: Harvest House Publishers, 2017).

SESSION ONE

1. Paul David Tripp, "Wednesday Word: A Weekly Devotional with Paul Tripp," *Paul Tripp Ministries, Inc.*, March 13, 2013, accessed April 3, 2020, https://www.paultripp.com/wednesdays-word/posts/talking-to-yourself.

2. *Dictionary.com*, s.v. "orthopraxy," accessed April 3, 2020, https://www.dictionary.com/browse/orthopraxy.

3. *Dictionary.com*, "ortho-." accessed April 3, 2020, https://www.dictionary.com/browse/ortho-.

4. *Dictionary.com*, s.v. "praxis," accessed April 3, 2020, https://www.dictionary.com/browse/praxis.

5. *Dictionary.com*, s.v. "orthodoxy," accessed April 3, 2020, https://www.dictionary.com/browse/orthodoxy?s=t.

6. Mark Allan Powell, "Historical Background," *Introducing the New Testament: A Historical, Literary, and Theological Survey*, (Grand Rapids, MI: Baker Academic, 2009).

7. Craig A. Evans, *The Bible Knowledge Background Commentary: John's Gospel, Hebrews–Revelation* (Colorado Springs: Cook Communications Ministries, 2005), 361.

8. Strong's G4137, *Blue Letter Bible*, accessed April 3, 2020, https://www.blueletterbible.org/lang/lexicon/lexicon.cfm?page=2&strongs=g4137&t=kjv#lexResults.

SESSION TWO

1. Simons, *Gracelaced: Discover Timeless Truths Through Seasons of the Heart*, 13.

2. A. W. Tozer, *Knowledge of the Holy* (Indo-European Publishing, reprint, 2018), 1.

3. Saint Augustine, "Book I," *The Confessions of Saint Augustine* (Irvine, CA: Xist Publishing, 2015).

4. Robert Robinson, "Come, Thou Fount of Every Blessing," 1758, https://hymnary.org/text/come_thou_fount_of_every_blessing.

5. Strong's G3870, *Blue Letter Bible*, accessed April 17, 2020, https://www.blueletterbible.org/lang/lexicon/lexicon.cfm?t=kjv&strongs=g3870.

6. "Heart," *Baker's Evangelical Dictionary of Biblical Theology*, ed. Walter A. Elwell, (Grand Rapids, MI: Baker Books, 1996), via BibleStudyTools, accessed April 17, 2020, https://www.biblestudytools.com/dictionary/heart/.

7. Charles Spurgeon, *The Complete Works of C. H. Spurgeon, vol. 58, Sermons 3283 to 3334* (United States of America: Delmarva Publications, Inc., 2013).

SESSION THREE

1. Simons, 65.

2. Bruce B. Barton, "Colossians 1:24–2:23," *Life Application Bible Commentary: Philippians, Colossians, & Philemon* (United States of America, Tyndale, 2016), 190, retrieved from https://app.wordsearchbible.lifeway.com.

SESSION FOUR

1. Simons, 119.

2. "NASB Bible Lexicon: Colossians 3:2," *Bible Hub*, accessed May 11, 2020, https://biblehub.com/lexicon/colossians/3-2.htm.

3. "NASB Bible Lexicon: Philippians 4:8," *Bible Hub*, accessed May 11, 2020, https://biblehub.com/lexicon/philippians/4-8.htm.

SESSION FIVE

1. Simons, 171.

2. Strong's G2716, *Blue Letter Bible*, accessed May 13, 2020, https://www.blueletterbible.org/lang/lexicon/lexicon.cfm?t=kjv&strongs=g2716.

3. Strong's G4342, *Blue Letter Bible*, accessed May 13, 2020, https://www.blueletterbible.org/lang/lexicon/lexicon.cfm?t=kjv&strongs=g4342.

FLOURISH IN HIS TRUTH

Be encouraged and inspired by
Ruth Chou Simons' gorgeously illustrated
meditations on the wonder of God's promises.

Visit **RuthChouSimons.com**
to discover the rest of her beautiful collection

Get the most from your study.

DVD Set includes 7 video teaching sessions from Ruth Chou Simons, each approximately 10 minutes

IN THIS STUDY, YOU'LL:

- Embrace what God says about you through a pattern of preaching the gospel to your heart in every season.

- Meet your trials and challenges with the truth of what is unchanging in Christ.

- Renew your heart and transform your mind by replacing self-talk with gospel truth.

To enrich your study experience, consider the accompanying *TruthFilled* video teaching sessions, approximately 10 minutes, from Ruth Chou Simons.

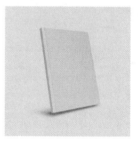

Teen Girls' Bible Study Book, includes 7-session study

STUDYING ON YOUR OWN?

Watch Ruth Chou Simons's teaching sessions, available via redemption code for individual video-streaming access, printed in this Bible study book.

LEADING A GROUP?

Each group member will need a *TruthFilled* Bible Study Book, which includes video access. Because all participants will have access to the video content, you can choose to watch the videos outside of your group meeting if desired. Or, if you're watching together and someone misses a group meeting, she'll have the flexibility to catch up! A DVD set is also available to purchase separately if desired.

Browse study formats, a free session sample, video clips, church promotional materials, and more at

lifeway.com/truthfilled